"Lizanne is an amazing woman with a deep message and contribution to our world. We are more than fortunate to embrace her as sister in our planet's process of Awakening, in which each of us plays an essential role. On any transformational journey, individual or collective, we are each charged with becoming global citizens. Doing so entails discovering our Original Wisdom from the Sacred Feminine, drawing from it a basis on which to serve Love incarnated. We are, as a humanity, charged with such a Love Project. Lizanne is such a steward."

~Dr. Cara Barker, carabarker.com, World Weary Woman: Her Wound and Transformation (Inner City 2001), "The Love Project: Coming Home" (University Press, 2012), "Grieving the Loss of a Child" (Sounds True), "Reclaiming the Sacred Feminine" (Sounds True), and more

"Lizanne is a powerful messenger who brings the Divine Feminine alive in our lives. Her words are beautiful and profound and serve to normalize the different legs of our journeys. She is like a candle that illuminates the way for the rest of us. As our companion, her words light our path and help us know that we are not alone. Our world is out of balance and desperately needs the influence of the feminine. Night Star is powerful enough to help us balance ourselves inside, which ultimately leads to balance in the outer *world. These beautifully written, eloquently expressed pieces are each a shining light for our own journeys. Reading this glorious book transports the reader to a different place inside. That place is called 'HOME.'"*

~Paula Jayne Friedland, LCSW, Certified Coach, public speaker and performing artist

"I am awed by Lizanne's transformational journey and her ability and willingness to share it — a realization that in letting go of the old there is a promise, a gift of new life, insight and strength. The path of the Divine Feminine provides markers of inspiration, as well as a roadmap and tools that give us hope and encouragement along our way. This is an eloquent, wise and inspiring book. It lifts and moves and opens one to a new level of understanding and appreciation of our life's potential."

~Barbara Harlow Nielson, Organizational Performance and Leadership Consultant

"The depth of emotion that comes through these gracefully written and emotionally powerful reflections is breathtaking. Lizanne's writings are a beautiful reminder that every day she guides women in both deeply personal and deeply spiritual journeys. We were not even aware that we needed these words until we read them, so thank you."

~Kerry Huberty, ABD, M.A., Instructional Developer, e-Learning and Online Pedagogy and Assessment, University of Wisconsin, Oshkosh

"Night Star *is anchored in the rich extraordinary depth of Lizanne's experience in being an authentic "midwife of the spirit." This is an essential book in the "curriculum of soul life" to guide and nurture the feminine transformational cycle of change and growth. The beauty and elegance of Lizanne's poetry inspires deep meaningful introspection. The co-creation of bringing the Divine Mother's message to the world is a true blessing and gift of love and wisdom."*

~Gail Haun, RN, MS, MCC, CCM, President of Potential Unlimited, Personal and Professional Life Coach, Health and Wellness Coach

"Night Star *is a compilation of spiritual speak that invites you to travel through the spirit of time as you meet the different aspects of the feminine soul. From death and rebirth to a resurrection coveted, Lizanne forges through the muck and unending beauty of the psyche, bringing it alive through her poetry and prose. I hope you take the time to converse with every stage of the feminine represented in this book because if you do you will be transformed. The simplicity allows for the sheer depth of the feminine psyche to be exposed with thoughtful, provoking and heartfelt integrity."*

~Edy Nathan, LCSW, Grief and Spirituality Retreat Facilitator, As seen on A&E's "Psychic Kids: Children of the Paranormal"

"Lizanne Corbit's powerful book Night Star, like the ancient myths and stories passed down through ages, provides a roadmap for traversing chthonic, dark, and desolate realms of the descent, death, rebirth and resurrection stages of the Feminine Way. Lizanne's poetry expresses the profound shifts and changes that occur in each phase of this feminine journey of transformation. Although we must ultimately travel this very challenging road alone, we find there are voices, maps, teachers, reminders and signs along the way. They bring us to a higher understanding of what it means to be accompanied by transpersonal forces that are not "seen" but experienced, felt, known. They remind us that this is the path to a deeper wisdom born of darkness — wisdom of the soul that cannot be achieved any other way. This book, and its guidance, offer waves of energy to carry the traveler through the domains of this complex, unpredictable and very difficult journey to rebirth and resurrection. I recommend that the reader take the time to read out loud the poetry and pay attention to the voices within that respond to each poem."

~Francesca Starr, Ph.D.,
Senior Voice Dialogue Coach and Trainer,
Founder Complete Life Center, Denver.
www.completelifecenter.com

The
NIGHT STAR

Lizanne Corbit M.A.

The Night Star:
Reflections on the Path of the Divine Feminine

Book Cover: Nick Zelinger
Editing: Donna Mazzitelli
Layout/Design: Andrea Costantine

Printed in the United States of America
First Edition
ISBN 13: 978-1-4820940-1-5
www.lizannecorbitcounselingdenver.com

The
NIGHT STAR

Reflections on the Path
of the Divine Feminine

Lizanne Corbit M.A.

DEDICATION

To the Divine Mother in all her shapes and forms.
May her deep abiding presence nourish
and nurture our souls.
May we allow her love to be the guiding
principle in how we live our lives.
She is the guiding light, the night star
ever present, ever bright,
seeking to be illuminated in our hearts and
enacted through our souls.
May her return bless us and guide us
in remembering her ancient ways.
May she foster the creation of a new way of relating
to each other and our planet, where we value each
other's goodness, wisdom, and truth,
and where we honor our body wisdom
through the nourishing and nurturing of
our soul gifts.
May we feel her grace and be empowered
by her presence.
For she has been, is, and will always be, present.
All we have to do is go inside, quiet our mind,
open our heart,
and listen from our soul.
May we hear her always.

CONTENTS

A Note From the Author

I ask myself why. Why write this book? Why share these reflections with others? The answer comes in a quiet but powerful voice that says, "I charge you with this task."

And of course I ask who is charging me with this undertaking. The answer once again comes, "I am your Mother and I am the light of the world. I am returning to this world in love for all, in guidance along the way and in beauty revealed."

I ask myself, "Have I lost my mind?" and the answer is "No. You are simply conveying an age-old message that must be remembered once more."

It is not my message that I share, but rather, it is the message of the Divine Feminine. When she speaks I listen, for she has been my saving grace throughout the cycles of death and rebirth my entire life. In respect and gratitude, and out of love and respect for her sacred presence, I offer to bring her message to light.

My understanding of the cycle of death and rebirth comes from my lineage. Having grown up in Walhalla, a small farming community in North Dakota, I was raised as all kids are who grow up in rural farm communities, with a deep respect and sense of the cycles of life. My mother and father farmed when I was young and most of my extended family are still farmers. I lived a direct experience of every changing season, and with it, participated in various tasks that were necessary to be performed according to the time of year...

Spring meant it was time to plow and make the soil ready for the planting of seeds. Summer represented the time of year to tend the crops and pray that Mother Nature would tend them as well and not destroy them with too much rain, wind, or dryness. Fall was the time of year when the fruits of our labors were hopefully harvested in ample time before the freeze set in. Winter brought the cold — the time when the ground froze and we returned home to repair and prepare for the coming spring. I came to know the cycles of death and rebirth first through Mother Nature.

As a young adult I searched for the meaning of life. I knew there had to be more, more than what I was aware of. It was through school and personal growth adventures that I was introduced to the cycle of change as an ancient process. I was fortunate enough to be guided to experience Holotropic Breathwork, by Stanislav Grof, M.D., a shamanic altered states process that uses breath and music to experience transpersonal states. For the next 25 years, I experienced firsthand the death and rebirth process. As a psychotherapist, being guided and guiding others through this powerful process of death and rebirth has been a gift and a treasure to behold.

But like all gifts, at least in the inner world, they come with a toll that must be paid. The price paid was extracted from me in the blood, sweat, and tears of doing my personal work. I entered another phase of growth and was divinely guided to Dr. Cara Barker and her book, *World Weary Women: Her Wound and Transformation*. I have spent the last 13 years of my life being taught how to reclaim and rebalance myself – my inner sovereignty – and align and live as best I can from the center of the "quaternity" of feminine archetypes, as is so well taught by Dr. Barker. It is a lifelong task, done over and over again – this tempering and testing from life's trials and challenges have taught me how to listen and hear the Divine Feminine wisdom through my body and from my soul. She has guided me through the Feminine Cycle of Transformation and midwifed me in the death and rebirth process. The price paid has always been worth the wisdom gained.

Throughout my lifetime I have studied, sought out, and received guidance from the Divine Feminine. Her form has changed depending on where I have been in my life at the time. As a child, she was Mother Mary. At times, she has been Sophia, or Shekinah, or Inanna. At other times, she has been Kwan Yin or Kali. During different phases in my life, she has been represented by different forms, but no matter her form, she has always been a guiding presence that soothed me along the way.

She has written to and through me, imploring that we understand the cycle of transformation – the death and rebirth cycle – and that women and men know the process and participate in it intentionally, consciously choosing care and compassion for ourselves, as we not only travel this journey personally but as we experience the death and rebirth cycle on a planetary level as well.

We are being called to become more than a "power over" culture. We are being asked to rebirth an empowering way of living, one where we support and cooperate; partner and collaborate; honor, respect, and value each other and all that we contribute to the world. Knowing the process of change and committing to support each other and ourselves through it is the path of the feminine way.

There has been enough war inside of us and in our world. It is time for a conscious change, where we choose love, care, and compassion as the guiding principles. She is calling for this change, and the death and rebirth cycle of transformation is the way through to our goodness. Inner change is what will transform outer change in the world. This map of the feminine cycle of transformation, when done with care and concern, love and compassion, is where the change begins. It begins with each of us embracing wherever we find ourselves in the cycle – descent, death, transformation, resurrection, or rebirth. Each stage has its invitation to learning and its accompanying challenges. Our job is to embrace the cycle at every stage and grab all the learning we can out of each, no matter how deep the descent.

The work required is designed to challenge us to

know ourselves in a way that we can act in accordance with our gifts, not our wounds. When we honor our gifts and live from this soul place, we bring the best of us to the world to be lived into and from. That is what we are asked to do. That is what the Divine Feminine is asking of us, to live the death and rebirth process consciously, helping ourselves and each other live from balancing our goodness with the human condition.

The Mother has been with me in times of trouble throughout my life, offering her guidance, her love, and her blessings along the way. It has been a lifetime of living through this cycle over and over again. It has been a lifetime of learning that this is a normal, natural process. It has been a lifetime of teaching others that they are experiencing something as old as time, an ancient process that has been going on forever and ever. It has been a lifetime of coming home and listening to the inner voice that guides me through this process with her wisdom and love. It has been a lifetime of honoring the crises and the gifts gleaned from the surrendering, the letting go, and the deathing part of the process. It has been a lifetime of claiming the blessings and pulling them out of the woundedness, transforming them into the resurrection and rebirthing part of the cycle. At times it has felt as if all was lost — peace, happiness, joy, value, competence, confidence never to be found again — only to be reminded that all is never lost. All is simply shifting and changing.

We need to let go in order to search for the deeper

truth of who we are, for we will die and be reborn many times in our one lifetime. It is an easier time of it when we know this is a part of the human condition that we have been experiencing for millennia. We are the change in the world.

It is with this knowing that I invite you to embrace your learning, your work, your stage on the cycle of transformation and seek out safe support in this sacred process. I invite you to travel to a place where you can be soul tended and learn to soul tend yourself so that the gift of who you are may be claimed as it was meant to be – as your birthright.

May the Mother of us all speak to you and provide for you throughout your lifetime all that you might need along your way, for she is forever and always present for us. All you have to do is ask and then listen for the quiet voice within – for she is the whisper in the wind. May she give you all that and more.

Blessings to you along your path,
Lizanne

Prologue

This is a manifestation of the Mother's anointment of me.

I have been guided to honor the feminine mystical path and female mystics such as Julian of Norwich, St. Theresa of Avila, Joan Of Arc, St. Catherine of Genoa, and St. Katherine of Sienna, to name a few.

I have been guided to honor the feminine tradition that models regeneration after death for those who came before me and those who will come after.

I have been guided since I was a child by the Feminine in her spiritual warrior state, in her loving mother's embrace, in her medial woman imaginal realm, and in her home and hearth body wisdom ways.

My heart and soul have been challenged, nurtured, nourished, and magically blessed by the ancestors before me, by the women who listened for spirit speaking through their hearts and souls, and I am honored to have them as teachers, guides, and my ancestry.

The Feminine way is true, rich, loving, and pure. It is challenging, tempering, sacrificing, and renewing. It is as old as time and honoring in its cyclical nature.

We are blessed as she, the Divine Mother, is

resurrected from the discarded and set in her rightful place once again. We are blessed to be of this time. We are blessed by her return. May we embrace her presence as a child would a long-lost mother.

Our ancestry is being reclaimed as we speak. We are love. We are loved. We are blessed. We are Divine. Let us remember our origins, our way through the dark and fearful places, and travel home to our truth.

Blessings to you along your way.

INTRODUCTION

Our lifetimes represent an ongoing process of death and rebirth. It is our human condition to experience change throughout our lives. We may experience it in the physical outside world, such as through relocation, disease, death of a loved one, divorce, or some other type of challenge. No matter what we undergo, we will experience it as change.

Most of us honor the hero's journey. Joseph Campbell spoke about this in his book, A Hero with a Thousand Faces. In his work, he studied the mythology of many cultures in the world. The hero's journey is characterized by hearing a calling, leaving what you know, meeting the challenges, trials, and tests along the way, and then returning to the world with the gifts acquired and sharing them with the world to make it a better place. We see this journey in all cultures, and in our western culture, we honor it in the stories shared by the returning hero, especially for the soldier returning from a tour of duty who survives and lives to tell the tale or the young teenage girl who is attacked by a shark while she is surfing and survives to not only live another day, but to inspire others with her story.

What we don't see in the hero/heroine's journey is that everyone lives this journey every day of our lives. Especially the Feminine journey, this does not take place in the outer world. Rather, it is of the inner world, where the challenges, tests, and crises are met in a much quieter way. The Feminine journey is less outwardly dramatic, but nonetheless, it is a struggle for life, where our challenge can be as basic as getting up every day and functioning even when it feels as if our world is falling apart. The struggle we don't see is the inner one that demands change from the inside out.

The challenges we don't immediately see can be the loss of an identity that we thought we would always have, the loss of our loved ones early in life without warning, the grief over the loss of our livelihood and not knowing how we are going to survive without a job, or the loss of our faith in ourselves because we no longer see or know who we are. These are the challenges we all face at one time or another during our lifetimes.

The hero/heroine's journey is our human condition. We will all travel it more than once. With love, compassion, hope, courage, strength, and empowerment, we can and do come through these journeys and all of their accompanying challenges each and every time. As a result of the hero/heroine's journey, we can and will not only survive but thrive, as so many of us have demonstrated with empathy for, championing of, cooperation with, and caring for others when it would have been just as easy to not do any of the above.

Our will works for the good of each and the good of all during these times of challenge. It is a choice we make in the midst of the crisis – to help our fellow man and woman and therefore help ourselves and our world.

My journey has been one of honoring the Feminine Path, which is a path of descent and rebirth – descent into and through the loss, crisis, test, trial, challenge, and the rebirth of our essence and our gifts into the world. We travel this path many times in our lifetime, each and every time returning with clarity of purpose, ownership of essence, and honoring of our soul, bringing with us into the world the gift of being. It is our birthright to make manifest the person we are here to fully be. The process of feminine transformation is not only for females – it is the inner journey we all experience in life.

The feminine transformational process consists of five stations or stages. They are descent, death, transformation, resurrection, and rebirth. Each of these stages brings with it its own challenges and its own remedy to meet the challenge. Every culture in the world provides the way and the means for being held in and through this process. The mystics of old provided the roadmap based on their own experiences. St. John of the Cross was a contemporary of the female mystic St. Teresa of Avila during the 6th Century. In his writings, he first named this transformational process "the dark night of the soul."

The mystics of today can be found in psychotherapy offices, in personal growth workshops, and in meditation retreats, where we look for comfort and care in our own dark night experiences. This is a normal human condition where we all seek answers for what we are experiencing. We all seek comfort in the disarray of our lives, guidance for our trials, and meaning for the unknown in order to find the truth and beauty of who we are, hoping to find our goodness in the middle of the wounds we carry.

The journey for me has been held, guided, and soothed by my teachers who have loved me in and through to arrive at my holiness and wholeness. It is the love, soothing, and guiding of the feminine path that fosters cooperation, collaboration, and partnership as the way to maneuver through the dark night of the soul journey.

The feminine way is being called to manifest in our world today. It is being created in our everyday lives, at those times when we have mercy, concern and care for, cooperation with, and understanding and empathy on behalf of another. At those times, we are able to change our inner world of loss, grief, confusion, despair, and loss of faith in ourselves and the world.

When we first demonstrate the feminine way to ourselves and then offer it to others, we become the change in the world. When we can manifest care and concern for ourselves, we can then demonstrate it to others. This is one of the lessons of the dark night journey — the feminine cycle of transformation — to learn to act in a caring way toward ourselves, which in turn teaches us how to act in this very same way with others. Our learning comes from being held by another in love, concern, and caring, when we ourselves are seen, soothed, and valued. As we come to experience our own value, we can value another. The feminine path is the guiding light in the darkness and through each stage along the way.

The feminine way is also the hope in the hopeless. It is the truth in the sacred cave of wisdom. It lives in each of us and can guide us to know our goodness, our essence, and our soul gifts here on earth.

We all want to feel our truth ringing loudly through our voices. We all want to be the person we were born to be. We all want to be seen, heard, and valued. We all want to be respected, empathized with, and treated fairly. We all want to feel competent and confident. And we all have a birthright to claim in our lifetime. The way to this knowing is to travel through the darkness to claim it at each stage as we are supported through the transformational journey by the feminine way.

Each of the following chapters represents a stage along the journey. The poems and writings were written from these stages, and I hope they speak to you and give you markers along the way that provide inspiration and hope as well as soothing and safety as you experience the journey yourself.

May the Divine Feminine bless you and keep you as you continue your travels along the feminine cycle of transformation.

CHAPTER ONE
THE JOURNEY

The sacred and ancient container of the Feminine Cycle of Transformation provides a framework for understanding and processing the challenges in the midst of crisis.

This transformational cycle consistently provides the mile marker for what stage we are in, as well as guidance for the tasks we need to meet and the skills we need to develop.

We have hope, reassurance, and comfort in the dark and chaotic, and often confusing times of our lives. That is what the journey provides — it gives us hope, a roadmap, and tools for traveling this age-old feminine path of transformation.

WE ARE THE ANCESTORS

We are the ancestors
We have been with you since before time
We sent you off on this journey
We have been with you ever since
We are light
We are love
We are your lineage
We bring you guidance
We are here to help
We love you
We bless you
We are your ancestors
You are here to bring light to darkness
Peace to despair
Love to aloneness
Joy to body
Everyone is dismembered
To remember to come closer to pure soulness
Journey in
Journey out
Journey around
Journey back
Journey to
Journey from

It is all
the journey to become
whole, holy and home
You are your Mother's Daughter
Blessings Dear One

THE WAY

The way is difficult yet alive with new life
The way is heart rendering yet speaks
volumes on love
The way is frightening yet provides the
way to move on
The way is challenging yet allows for
smooth sailing in
the midst of rough seas
The way is unnerving yet tended to
with soulful soothing

The way is
Through
Down
In
Around
Out
About

It is Encompassing
Enlivening
Empowering

Spirited
Soul grabbing
Self-polishing
Truth evoking

It is Life giving
Nourishing
Nurturing

Drink from the well of the Divine Feminine
For she will provide a safe haven, a respite from the
challenging world and nourishment for the soul

THE JOURNEY

This journey
From birth to death
It is a turn and return around the wheel of life
Sometimes like a newborn baby
so vulnerable and beautiful
full of life anew
Sometimes beaten down and broken
open to life's challenges
revealing just how strong you are
Sometimes whirling around in a vortex of change
dizzy from the unexpected tosses and turns
life throws at you
Sometimes sweet and soft as we land
in a warm loving embrace
of the place we feel inside is home sweet home
Sometimes it is like worshiping in a cathedral
reveling in all the majesty and miracles
on this path we call life
Always knowing that whatever part of the
journey we are on it will be temporary
Until the next step reveals the next gift, treasure,
blessing, challenge, hazard or test on the path

For we will continue to walk the path,
travel the terrain of change
and continue to turn and return
to this cycle of death and rebirth
until the end of our days
It is a blessed path for those willing
to know their truth
for those willing to let go of untruths
for those willing to embrace the dark and the light
for those willing to give back to the world their gifts
from their journey

The journey humbles yet strengthens
Challenges yet enlightens
Strips off yet empowers
Breaks apart yet consolidates
Confounds yet brings clarity
Silences yet solidifies
Deaths yet births anew
Struggles yet breathes new life
Lives on yet dies each day

Am I?

Child of mine
Everyone must tell their story
Everyone must be heard
Everyone must be held in their vulnerability
Everyone must be seen in their goodness
Everyone!
Everyone is vulnerable here in this life
Everyone deserves kindness bestowed upon them
Everyone desires to be known
at the very core of their being
Everyone yearns for love guidance and peace
Everyone craves blessings and goodness freely given
Everyone makes mistakes and everyone deserves to be
forgiven, not everyone can forgive
or receive forgiveness and for them we send love to
heal their hardened hearts
Everyone seeks their goodness in their life, some are
fortunate enough to have it mirrored back to them
in the faces of others
Some never see their beauty reflected back to them
and for them we pray for an inkling of knowing
Everyone desires to know their deepest design
They may recognize it when they see it or it may be
too close to them and they mistake it for the mundane
rather than the magic that it really is

Everyone challenges themselves every minute of every
day to balance the opposites
Am I good Am I bad?
Am I sweet Am I sorrow?
Am I kind Am I cruel?
Am I loving Am I hate-filled?
Am I blessed Am I cursed?
Am I humble Am I arrogant?
Am I sane Am I insane?
Am I clever Am I crazy?
Am I saint Am I sinner?
Am I soul Am I human frailty?
Am I sound Am I unstable?
Am I genuine Am I afraid?
Am I deserving Am I defective?
Am I God or Goddess's child?
Am I?
I am the question and I am the answer
I am the choice and the living into it
I am the challenge and the meeting it
I am the within each and all
I am the light and the dark
I am the heavens and the earth
I am the spirit and the matter
I am the aliveness and the breath
I am the energy that brings the dance of life into
form
Alive with duality and choice

In every minute of every day you get to choose ME!
Bringing yourself into alignment with your goodness
and humanness but every day you must choose

I pray that you choose
love over hurt
truth over wounds
faith over fear

faith in yourself
our world
and
each other
that is what I pray for!

SOPHIA

Sophia, Our Divine Feminine,
She returns us to our deepest truth
She creates space within so our beauty can flourish
She blesses us and soothes us as we return
from the challenges of living life
She holds us lovingly so we can embody our essence
She fiercely guards our vulnerability and innocence
She guides us in the deep quiet with her holy wisdom

We are here on this human journey to embody our
divinity, as we have been originally blessed
and as so often happens on this journey
we forget our deepest truth—we are divine in nature.

The feminine is our passageway. Through her we
embody our light, our truth and our essence. She
brings us home to find the—instatus nascendi—the
jewels hidden within matter. Experience the sweetness
of the Great Mother as we honor the Divine Feminine
in each and all and learn to hold ourselves, each other
and the world from this place of holy wisdom.

The Divine Feminine births us into existence,
allow her holy wisdom to birth you.
You are here to be her, who is she,
you are meant to be.

Thank Goodness Goddess

I am living the truth that has always been there
It does not determine my value
it just speaks to my truth
That all beings are divine and we are all provided for
and we all are wounded
and we all have the opportunity to live into
and through the woundedness
To the truth   To our soulfulness
My journey has seemed to be this living into
and going through the wounded
Shedding its reality, its skin and acquiring my inner
gifts, truth, soulfulness, essence, authentic,
divine aspects of who I am

Leave what you know
Experience a crisis
Grow out of your limitedness
Acquire your gifts and truth
and come into the world anew
The Heroine's Journey

Go into the darkness and strip yourself or be stripped
of the old ways as you unite with yourself and move
to the marrow (life force) of your bones

Reattach and reassign yourself to your soul,
Realign with your deepest truth
Be seen, heard, felt and thus restored
Release what no longer serves you
Burn it
Compost it
Return it back to the Mother to feed the soul and
enrich the Universe

The wounds have served their purpose
The wounded has lived out its karmic agreement,
personal consciousness agreement, and now it is time
to release it, thank it and honor it
for its difficult due diligence duty
We are strong enough, mature enough and capable
enough to handle the let go of the wounds
and to own the truth
What is your deep truth? What is the deep truth that
you have been avoiding, struggling with,
disregarding, seeking, desiring, yearning for?
Are you ready? Are you courageous enough?
Are you willing to let go of your wounds and restore
your Self to its rightful place? To its sovereignty?
Allowing your voice to speak
To hear the truth in the midst of the chaos
and crisis inside
Let us seek the struggle and go into it
Feel it, release it and reclaim your rightful place in
your inner Queendom

Allow the deeper truth to emerge fully in you
Allow the struggle a place to release
Allow your spirit, body and soul a birthing canal for
your truth
to be rebirthed and received, seen and blessed

Miracles Mysticism & Magic

What do you have for me today dear death mother?

Miracles Mysticism and Magic
That is what I have for you today dear child of mine

Miracles to inspire hope
Mysticism to implore understanding
&
Magic to transform every day
Into beauty, hope and meaning making
&
the courage, reverence and mirth to live into every
day

Blessed be those that seek to know the wisdom that
lives in every cell of their body
Blessed be those that know the truth
of their soul's embodiment
Blessed be those that live from the deep abiding
inner genius of their soul's gifts
Blessed be those that hear the call to love,
embody the truth of ages,
live from the trust of being all that
they are born to be

Blessed be those that travel the path of change,
shed the skins of their old identity
and transform into the beauty
of their soul's embodiment
Blessed be those that Love others, Love themselves,
Love each other in this changing time
Blessed be those that sing their bones into being,
dance their ecstasy alive, allow their spirit to unfold
in an unending unfurling beauty

Blessed be those that allow
bless
&
be
the gift of being
they are here to be
alive in their goodness
their soulfulness
their beauty
Blessed Be
Thee

CHAPTER TWO
MOTHER'S BLESSINGS

In all the tales of old, when a traveler sets off on their peregrine, or travels, they are always sent off with a blessing.

What follows are the blessings sent to us by the Divine Mother for our safe travels throughout the Feminine Cycle of Transformation.

MOTHER MARY LOVING SOPHIA

Mother Mary Loving Sophia
I am here to heed your call
As a daughter I will take care
As a devotee I will serve you
As a woman I will bless you
As a spirit I will follow you

I am here fully present to be guided, held
and affirmed by you
I rest in your presence and love
I nourish myself with prayers to you
and for your presence in the world
to help heal the violence and chaos within myself
and with others

Love Thy Self and commit to live compassionately
with yourself and others

Beauty is being surrounded by spirit beings
guiding and helping me be my soul-filled self
Beautiful too is the love I feel from them
as they walk in unison with me
loving me every step of the way
Beauty is your presence
Beautiful too is your love

Mother Mater Ma

Mother Mater Ma
Wherever there is Love you are
Wherever there is Compassion you are
Wherever there is Mercy you are
Wherever there is Joy you are
Wherever there is Kindness you are
Wherever there is Redemption you are
Wherever there is Grace you are
Wherever there is Prayer you are
Wherever there is Suffering you are
Wherever there is Faith you are
Wherever there is Laughter you are
Wherever there is Honor you are
Wherever there is Peace you are
Wherever there is Integrity you are
Wherever there is Reverence you are
Wherever there is Strength you are
Wherever there is Wisdom you are
Wherever there is Protection you are
Wherever there is Eternity you are
Wherever there is Breath you are
Wherever there is Intuition you are
Wherever there is Beauty you are
Wherever there is Blessings you are

Mother Mater Ma
You are in all things alive with pulsating energy
Bringing us alive in all ways
Blessing us in your nourishing way
Our bodies
Our souls
Our spirits
And our place on the planet
You prove your existence every day
by shining your light
for us to see in all these ways

In gratitude
Thank you

Dearest Light of the World

MOTHER MARY

Mother Mary
I am so abidingly aware of her presence
It surprises me and yet not
She communicates through me and speaks to me
She has been forever present since I was young
I have prayed to her for years
As a child for intercession
As an adult for comfort and solace
As a woman for peace and soothing
As a person for guidance and strength
She has given me all of these things
in all times of my life
She is the beauty and the light in the energy
freely given in each of the gifts she gives to us
in her soothing
her guidance
her comfort
her presence

She is the aliveness in the comfort felt
in a loving exchange
She is the lightness felt in the spring breeze
She is the warmth in the warm embrace

She is the breath in the first gasp of air
of a newborn baby
She is the sustenance in the food shared in a meal
She is the brightness in the sun shining down on us
She is the sweetness in the birthday cake
especially made for you
She is the comforting hand on your back
as you weep in sorrow
She is the aliveness in your eyes
when you laugh out loud
at whatever has struck your fancy
She is the spirit surrounding you
as you pray for peace
She is the holy embracing you as you birth your soul
She is the beauty
of being a living breathing human being

Know your source is me

She who brings love into form
She who brings blessings to you
She who graces you with guidance
And she who loves everlasting and unending you
forever and always
Amen

DEAREST CHILD

Dearest child
I walk among you
I walk between you
I walk in the mist-filled path

I share my love with you
I share my wisdom with you
I share my energy with you

I weave the spells that create new life
I raise the energy to make manifest visions
I conjure up the spirits to support souls embodying

I pray for the good of all
I bless the good in each
I love beauty into being

I am forever
I am eternal
I am everlasting
I am infinite
I am Divine

Embodied in all living things
Uniquely Sweetly
Allowingly Blessedly
Alive!

THE MOTHER'S LOVE

Blessed be dear child
you are my daughter
here to make me available for others
to hear my message of love
Love is everlasting
Love lives in your intent
Love lives in every action
Love lives in all energy
Love is the way, the truth and the light
It lights the way in the darkest of nights
It warms even the coldest of hearts
It soothes even the most alone and abandoned
It calms even the most raging of storms
It nurtures even the smallest
of Mother Nature's creatures
It envelopes even the biggest and most powerful
energies on the planet
It inspires us to connect in love
with the beauty in another human being
Love Love Love
Love sustains
Love creates
Love embraces
Love hears

All the cries for help
Pleas for saving grace
Petitions for new life
Prayers for salvation
Demands trying to invoke
a miracle where one is needed

Mother Mary is love
She responds with a whisper to hear and listen for
an act of beauty to be seen and looked for
a blessing in the form of creation
to be awed and anticipated
a miracle in the midst of chaos
to be graced with and soothed ever so sweetly
a beauty that inspires us and calls us to act in love
a sweetness that nourishes and at the same time
calms our weary souls
She invokes encourages enlivens
the very fabric of our being
We will be blessed by her every minute of every day
If we choose to bow in reverence
and love to her majestic presence
in every and all for evermore
Our Loving Mother's Blessing Is Love
Amen

The Way of Blessing

Ours is the way of Blessing
Blessing Blessing Blessing
Blessed Beloved Beauty of who you are
Each and every one of you hold the key to becoming
Becoming all that you were sent here to be
Children of God
Alive in holiness
Alive in blessedness
Alive in goodness
Being human is a challenge and a gift
You choose how you receive it and what you do with it
You decide how to receive the teachings
you are here to learn
Everyone learns and everyone leaves
the realm of spirit to come here
to further their learning and their soul development
Some remember some forget
Some embrace some repel
Some live some die as part of their growth
Some know some never know the beauty
of who they are
Some give and receive and some never know the taste
of love upon their lips
Some remain ignorant to the beauty of their being
Some revel in the knowing of their sacredness

All beings struggle
All beings are challenged
All beings are broken apart
All beings are dismembered
All beings are opened up to receive new life
All beings retain the divine origins they came in with
All beings live a lie that they are not enough
until they arise and reclaim their divine origins
All beings have the opportunity many times over to
embrace their true nature
All beings are loved by God
All beings!!

GRACE GRANTED

Good morning Dear One
This morning I awake and feel the quiet
And it feels soft and serene this early morning quiet
I hear and feel the presence of the Divine in me and
feel grateful for my life and the beautiful presence
This presence this glow within
is the Divine Presence in all things
The Deep Energy alive in all things
Mary the Mother and Mary the daughter
alive in all things
Energy and spirit together intermingling in me,
as me, is me

Thy beauty rests in my soul
Thy beauty runs in my veins
Thy blessedness showers me with grace
I am your daughter Queen of the Stars
Devoted to embodying your light here on earth and
in my body and soul
My life is a reflection of your facets

The fall
the redemption
the resurrection
eucharist
and communion
I am a reflection of your grace granted

MOTHERS

Mothers are homes
Home to gestating life
Home to the newly born
Newborn babies
Ideas
Visions
Beings
They hold, warm, contain
nourish, nurture, sustain
they provide, protect and promise a better future

Woe is the Mother
For she will raise her children
and have to let them go
but still carry all the love for them
as long as they are alive in their hearts
forever watching
holding from afar
encouraging ever so slightly
exerting influence carefully
allowing gracefully
Mothers bless whole-heartily
Challenge appropriately
Presence themselves lovingly

Mothers come in all shapes and sizes
To create
Nourish
And
Bless their children

Whether it be a child, a vocation, a process,
a project or a person
They avail their energy for
the creation of whatever they are here to create
They feed energy to the creation
and provide sustenance until it can sustain itself
They forever guard their creations
to protect their vulnerability and soul essence
for they see it as no one else may
They provide a safe container
in which and from which
to enter and retreat from the weary world
They are the energetic fabric that holds the world
together
Strongly sweetly
Weaving the web of universal energy
Holding us everlasting evermore
In love eternal

CHAPTER THREE
DESCENT

*This is the first stage in which we find ourselves
during the Feminine Cycle of Transformation.*

*We descend into the unknown. We surrender to the
fear as we strip off our old identity.
We live in the chaos of change.*

*We learn to slow down, seek support,
soothe ourselves in the challenge of the unknown,
and we seek guidance along the way.*

*We learn to listen for the still,
small voice inside to guide us onward.
We pray for peace.*

*We receive all of this when we slow down our pace and
listen to the inner rhythm of our inner life that calls for
us to quiet ourselves.*

SPINNING

Spinning spinning crazily spinning
In and out and around
Your truth, your essence, your beauty
Within cannot land only spin
Around, within, without
below, above, but not within
within is where the peace lies
within is where the stillness sits
within is where the groundedness resides
within is where the truth lives
within is where the everlasting spirit rests
within cannot be reached while in the spin
therefore all feels lost chaotic frenetic
sad hopeless and fearful
within can be found when a deep breath is taken
over and over again until the heart calms
and the body feels soothed to quietness
where energy slows down and calm whispers,
"all is going to be OK"
within the within lies the sweet words of wisdom
offering all the craziness up for our highest good
to be pulled through the eye of the needle
and sewn into the fabric of our being

within the within echoes with wisdom's words
of sorrow for your loss of faith
in yourself and your beauty
within the within quietly awaits the arrival
of your senses
hearing feeling tasting touching the truth
that you are more than your wounds
within the within aliveness awaits
its anchoring to be steadfastly
connected to your essence

Within

TEARS OF EMPTINESS

Crying tears of emptiness
Aloneness
In the darkness everlasting
Eternal
Loss
Lost in the emptiness
Deadened imploding
Severe
Sever
Sinking
Senses
Self
Soul
Sick in sentiment
Sacrament
Sacrifice
Sentient
Who is in this emptiness?
You are
in the emptiness of sacrifice!
It is the emptiness of
loss
It is the emptiness of searing
aloneness

It is the emptiness of vacant
senses
It is the emptiness of undying
deathing
It is the emptiness of simple
nonexistence
It is the emptiness of the holes
in your heart
It is the emptiness of radical
sacramental sacrifice
It is the emptiness of spirits
silenced
It is the emptiness of devoid
emotions

It is the emptiness of my soul screaming
for manifestation of being that has yet to be birthed
It is the silent swirling of atoms called into form to
create anew the being yet to be born

Sit in the silence, let the emptiness engulf you fully
so you may hear the mystery singing
its psalms to you

The Invocation of Creation

Of What Do I Seek?

Of what do I seek?
Solitude to quiet my mind
Silence to quiet my heart
Strength to listen deeply

I am anxious
Anxiously awaiting the arrival of my soul's direction
Instructions for my Self
Guidance for my soul
Steps to take
To get to where I am going
To acquire what I am to learn
Yet I am in no hurry
I like the quiet unknowing
I like the restful pause
I like the inner path
I like the beauty of the unknown
I like the pregnant nothingness

I sit in the wee small hours of the morning
and hear the majestic trumpets
blare into the quiet
announcing the arrival of the stillness
revealing the majestic richness of nothingness

In the darkness lies the truth of ages
Can you lie here long enough to hear the truth or are
you too young to weather the eternal silence?

The silence used to be riddled with the constant
chatter of negative schemas.
"You are defective, unworthy, bad, alone, etc…"

Now it is filled with the rhythmic lullaby
of the Divine Mother
rocking me with her songs of soothing.
Holding me in the darkness as the waves of change
lap against my shores
Keeping me safe

Broken

Sometimes I feel the heaviness, the loss
and the grief and I get tired. I do feel broken inside
Something is broken in me not irreparable
but nonetheless broken
I am heartbroken sad heavy-hearted
guiding me to be careful with myself and others

Care for myself
Take care to caretake myself
and acknowledge my broken heart

It is broken

Out of the brokenness
Comes Tenderness
Comes Vulnerability
Comes Sadness
Comes Openness
Comes Heaviness
Comes Grief
Come Tears of Loss
Comes Gentleness
Comes Love
Comes Silence

Comes Solitude
Comes Mourning
Come Memories
Comes Gratitude
Comes Peace

Naked

The fearful harmful planetary energy I feel
I want to pull into a safe quiet place inside where
everything is OK again

the aloneness feels better
the quiet of the mystery soothes me
the reflection of the dark moonlit sky envelopes me
me and my god alone in the craziness
swirling around me
single focus,
to breathe from one moment into the next
keeping me tethered to the ground
recklessly, dangerously, loosely, flapping in the gale
force winds

The secret life of me
Deep dark descent into craziness
Unearthed, untethered, unconscious made conscious
by the ripping, shredding, tearing apart
any and all knowing of any previous sense of being

Anxious
Broken into tiny bits
Calling to be reassembled

Crying at the broken apart
Craving the wholeness anew
Anxiously awaiting the issuance
of the new working order

What is it?
I don't know, I am just anxiously waiting
Jumping out of my skin
Peeling off any and all oldness that doesn't fit me nor
the new working orders

Befitting a new queen is a new robe
that is not yet ready
So I stand naked and vulnerable,
having shed the old robe, torn and tattered
I await, nude, innocent and open,
the reveal of the new robe
Hurry Please!

Chapter Four
Death

*Here we begin the second stage in the
Feminine Cycle of Transformation.*

*We no longer feel the aliveness of our life.
Nothing is the matter, of course. No thing will bring
us the aliveness. It is the quieting of the senses that
will bring us peace, the slowing of the busy doing of
the outside world that will calm us.*

*It is the silencing of the busyness of the outside world
that allows for our beauty to be heard — not seen, but
heard in the far off distance.*

*Here is where we allow the old aspects of us to die,
to let go, to not know, to feel unraveled, as if we are
crawling out of our old skin.*

*Here is where we hold the tension of letting go with the
unknown and soothe the shattered old self with calm,
peace, and quiet.*

THE COFFIN

Deep within lies the coffin
Within the coffin lies the woman
She is spent and deadened to her senses
Lying quietly listening to her heart beat
Waiting for her life's blood to sing again
its siren song
calling her into life again

The wooden box is placed in mother earth
where she feels
The safety and soothing of her dark rich soil
Waiting resting rejuvenating

Acquiring the knowledge to move on,
move forward, to move within
to carry forth the purpose bestowed upon her
Of which she has always acted on in life
Offering meaning to the meaningless
Offering love to the unloved
Offering guidance to the lost ones

She is the midwife who is being birthed anew
Through each contraction she breathes
and struggles forth

Shedding the coffin
The dead skin of the old life
Peeling off sloughing off
the old personhood
The wounded life, the unfulfilling patterns,
the old beliefs and unconsciousness
that will no longer serve her in her new body

Her new self not yet emerged
but molting in the coffin container

Thank God! I am being held in this process
Thank you great Mother for midwifing me in this
Death and yet-to-be Resurrection

Death Mother

What do you have for me today Dear Death Mother?

I am here to remind you of the underworld
where it is necessary to return in order to redeem,
reclaim, release, remember
the most important parts of who you are

Soulfully and spiritually connect
with your richer truth
that is birthed in the cave of wisdom
Under the light of the moon
illuminated by the Mother
who cares for you in this
despairing brokenness in the depths of your being

Broken Broken
Abidingly broken
Rewritten
Realigned
Remembered
In the spiritual marrow of your bones

Reweaving
Reimprinting
Resourcing
With the universal truths in your soul's DNA

Freeing you from the shackles
of the past that have bonded you
to a cycle of Death

Death of your
Energy
Death of your
Spirit
Death of your
Aliveness
Death of your
Receptacle of New Life
Death of your
Peace
Death of your
Loving
Death of your
Compassion
Death of your
Heartfeltness
Death of your
Feminine Nature

The iron shackles have worn you out
tired you beyond belief
broken your spirit

Now that you are at choice again
you can be in the aliveness
or deadness of this exact moment
You are forever the Spiritual Warrioress
Slaying dragons
Battling the negative masculine
In his sorcery
Cutting the untruths away one limb at a time
with your swords and daggers
Exacting truth where it is buried in the dark and
dangerous caverns
Surrounded by the
Demons of
Self-doubt
Shame
Criticalness
And despairing screams, "THAT YOU ARE
ALONE ALWAYS!"

You dare enter the underworld
Knowing you will be stripped bare
naked and vulnerable beyond belief
Fearing yet knowing
That this is
the way of Wisdom
the way of Soul
the way of Spirit

It is the only way to recover that which has been lost
Your Bruised and Bleeding
Heart
Soul and Feminine

For she is beyond the gates of hell
Beyond the brokenness
Beyond the fight
Beyond the most achingly naked
exposed vulnerability
Beyond the despair, sadness and aloneness
Beyond the tears of bloodied sacrifice

She is
that tiny light in the space between the sobs
She is
in the space between the dreams
that have been broken
She is
in the space between the rush of adrenaline
She is
in the space between the dark
and the darkest moment
She is
in the space between each tear as it drops
She is
in the space between each deep sigh of resignation
She is
in the space between

opening allowing soothing
softening resting loving
deserving blessing receiving

Glowing in the moonlit night
Showering me with her glittering moonlight
Reviving me on my deathbed with new life
Ever tender ever slight ever eternal and everlasting

She is the light that embraces me
and carries me forth
Regenerating me
Healing me
Recuperating me
Recovering me
One
limb
at
a
time...

Hear My Cries!

Dearest Daughter, hear me!

Hear my cries in the middle of the night
Hear my whispers in the wee hours of the morning

Hear my call to you to be love
in the depths of your despair
Hear my guidance in the nudge of your intuition

Hear my scream in warning that all will be lost
if we stop caring for one another

Hear my laugh with pure joy
as the beauty of the mystic
meets the mundane and turns it into magic

Hear me breathe a sigh of relief when tenderness
touches the vulnerable in another

Hear me cackle when someone pretends
to harness the secrets of the Universe
only to have Mother Nature remind them
of their place in it

Hear me chant blessings in the flowing
water of the raindrops
of the thunder and lightning storm

Hear me in the silence of your inner being
as I emerge
in an idea, thought, insight
or burst of creative energy

Hear me in your cries of sexual ecstasy
for creation is so close at hand

Hear me bellow for you to follow me
from your physical body into spirit form

Hear me delight in your love and devotion

My Daughter
My Devotee
My Delightful Devi

I Am Tired

I am tired of the fight
The fight to stay on top,
above
within
beyond
Sinking deeply into the muck and mire

Descent darkness aloneness
Destroying destruction devastation
Energy depleted
Aliveness defeated
Sludge invading my veins
Slowing down the life force to a
drudgingly monotonous pace

Deafening aloneness
Stillness echoing, reverberating
Silence stillness quiet
Alone lonely abandoned
to the aloneness of your existence

Goodnight!

Sinking
seeking
surrendering
to the physical depletion
death of my energy
life force
hope

Surrender to the devastatingly depleted body
Surrender to the inattentive behavior
that wounds me beyond measure
Surrender to the broken heart
that bleeds sadness
Surrender to the old reality
that speaks volumes on loneliness and abandonment
Surrender to the acts of exclusion
that reap defectiveness and sow shame
Surrender to the soul crying for the mother
to love it evermore in the midst
of this vacuum called existence

I exist in the midst of the aloneness
I exist in the midst of the depletion
I exist in the midst of the devastation
I exist in the midst of the loneliness
I exist in the breath of fresh air
I exist in the sigh of relief
I exist in the spaces between the heart breaking
I exist in the blink of an eye
I exist in the tension of holding on
I exist in the flex of a muscle
I exist in the cadence of a poem

I exist in the beat of a heart
I exist in the silence of hearing a pin drop

I exist in Thee!

No matter the devastation
depletedness, aloneness, vacuum
I still exist in the blood flowing through your veins

I hold the light for you as living snuffs out the flame
for this moment!
I guard the light so it may reignite another time and
bring warmth once again
to your weary bones and your broken heart!

I Am Dark and Beautiful

Dark is the flame of resurrection and sacrifice
Dark is the light of the Divine Feminine
Dark is the path of sacrifice and death
Dark is the inner illumination like a moonlit night
casting shadows here and there

Dark is the beauty that resides in this place of
consumption of my being
Dark is the nighttime of my self-evaluation
Dark is this place of peace within me

I am dark and beautiful and rich as loam soil
full of generative minerals bringing life
to seeds of truth

I am dark and beautiful like the night sky
illuminated by the majesty of the starlight

I am dark and beautiful containing ancient
markings and paintings
secured deep in the caves of mother earth

I am dark and beautiful benevolent black Madonna
showering grace and love on all who worship her
in the grotto of their souls

I am dark and beautiful Mother Mary
holding those who die in her arms
up to the heavens for blessings and guidance
on their journey

I am dark and beautiful the shamaness traversing
the spirit realm
collecting pieces of bone and fragments of souls to
return to their rightful owners

I am Dark and Beautiful
I am

I Live in the Darkness

I live in the darkness
I am living in the darkness of this life where sadness
grabs me and demands payment
for all the sorrows of my existence

I live in the darkness where the emptiness envelopes
my very being and leaves a single flame
as a reminder that darkness prevails

I live in the darkness where the voices
of love whisper words of despair
reminding me that the journey is worth the struggle

I live in the darkness where desuetude
drains my spirit
leaving me devoid of any energy
so I may contemplate my purpose

I live in the darkness
where depression sings its siren song
seducing me into my grief, my loss and my sadness
so I may feel this depth
and prepare me for the coming

I live in the darkness where spirit, soul and self
collude to death me in my unfitting state of being
and resurrect me from the flames of transmutation
to my rightful place

I live in the darkness gathering, sorting, grieving,
crying aloud for the beauty to return
and I am pulled deeper and deeper into the magic of
the blackness,
where all beauty begins life

I live in the darkness, the womb of the Mother,
Being held and fed and surrounded
with solitude and safety
as I form from the unformed unfolding spirit

I live in the Darkness of Living Life

UNDONE

Fragile Fragile Fragile
Shaking inside
My center is awry agog ajar
Shaking Shaking Shaking
Inside
Undone
Grasping for peace for calm for steady
Undone
Inside
deep fear deep peace
deep unraveling of old
unfurling of my center
Inside
Undone
I want the center that keeps me safe
Solid Sane Secure
Where have you gone?
I am swirling in the night
I am traveling in the universe
I am flying in the ethers
Not landed yet but unfurling around you
and the world
Opening to the Feminine who will wrap her powerful
life force around you all

And calm and soothe you until you are
Secure
Secure in the knowing
that peace will come again
love will reign
security will prevail
cooperation will be the key
unity will bring with it goodness
creation will birth anew
and we will rest in peace
Once again the Feminine will come to
manifest in our hearts and souls and
we will partner again with her on this Earth
She will bless us in our fear
She will calm us in our undone
She will soothe us in our fragile
She will guide us in our unfurling
She will love us in our newness
She will hold us in our unraveling
She will know us in our unknown
She will come to us in our naiveté
And bless us in our becoming
She forgives us in our humanness
and promises us a better time of it
Your undone unraveled unfurling is a releasing of the
feminine way into the world
Be blessed in her coming!

FAITH

Efforting! Efforting! Efforting!
What? What? What?

What
do you want from me?

I trust I have faith I practice I pray
I compel I teach I show up every day
What am I to do?
Just tell me, you tell me and I will do it,
be it, but you must tell me!

Go within
down
in
deeply align
with
Peace
Where does the peace come from you ask?
It comes from
Faith
Faith that you are OK
Faith that you are taken care of in a higher order
Faith that you have not been forsaken

Faith that deep inside you is worth
and goodness and peace
Faith that no matter what goes on
in the world you are safe
Faith that all is not for naught
but that all is for your greater good
Faith that within you lies
worth and value and deservedness
that can never be taken away unless you let it
Faith that there is a divine plan for your safety
and security and prosperity
Faith that this is all a part of the Heroine's Journey
Dark Night Travels and
the bigger plan of death and rebirth

Death your insecurity and replace it
with faith in the divine
Death your fear and replace it with faith in love
Death your hurt and replace it with faith in peace
Death your masculine and replace it
with Faith in the Mother
Death your anger envy jealousy and replace it
with faith in gratitude

Put your faith in practice
Put your faith in your being
Put your faith in the love of the Mother
Put your faith in the reweaving of your soul's DNA
Once again align the beauty with the Heaven on
Earth
Bring it in
Pull it down
Grab it fully
Live it consciously

CHAPTER FIVE
TRANSFORMATION

*We have now arrived at the third stage in the
Feminine Cycle of Transformation.*

*Here is where we begin to see the ray of light that
brings with it hope. In this hope we begin to discern
what has been stripped from our identity and what no
longer serves us.*

*Here, we discover our essence
that is to be preserved for our becoming.*

*We hear the voice strongly calling us to know our gifts,
truths, and soulfulness. We heed the call and begin to
lay claim to our truth and our birthright.
We experience the quiet magic that transforms us from
our wounded selves into our God-given Self.*

*We begin to honor what we see, love what we know,
and bless who we are as the gift we are here to be.
Here we pray to remember, reattach, and
realign with our deepest truth and sacred origins.*

DARK NIGHT MASK

My dark night mask crying tears of jewels
In each teardrop there is a gift of new life
In each teardrop there is a letting go of old life
and the grief of what it takes to be human
Knowing sadness, hurt, aloneness,
separation from the divine, fear, shame
And the beauty in this experience
where compassion is birthed
Coming alive as I recognize these in others
as the same in me
We are alike in our experiences of this humanness

The jewels are the beauty of who we are
in the body and flesh of our bodies
The spirit in the matter
The soul in the body ready to be polished, claimed,
cleaned of the fecal matter
that has buried them from sight
This alchemical spelunking is not
for the faint of heart!
The dark decaying life matter stinks, is rotting like
vegetation that has been decaying in the earth
It is renewing, it is luscious in its decaying form

The beads full of color are the new life
Not yet fully formed but filled
with the promise of beauty yet to come

The Raven is the harbinger of the underworld
The flying seer
Into the darkness able to maneuver in the underworld
because this is her domain
She covers my eyes with her feathers because I need
eyes to see and they are not my eyes
but the eyes of intuition, insight, clairvoyance, spirit
Soulful eyes that
Know without seeing
Feel into
Create from nothing
See in the darkness
Reveal the truth
Revel in the unknown
Hear the spirits talking
Are blinded by the darkness
yet see the beauty in the decay
That know, in the underworld things are topsy turvy
and that the darkness sweetly sings
its song of death
And that the ancestors
are dancing this death into life
I am blessed!

LET CREATION HAPPEN

I am in the liminal darkness asking once again
Who am I?
What is calling me?

Individuation is the journey
Wholeness is the gift
Darkness is the medium
In silence is the answer

Sit in silence
Let creation happen

Who am I at this moment?
What do I want?

Quiet
Solitude
Peace
Purpose
Direction

You have it, go within
Go into the quiet

I am the traveler on the journey
I have left what I have known and am walking the
path following the inner promptings

I walk
I sit
I run
I rest
I stop
I start

I steel myself against the vastness
of the opening ahead of me
I am excited for the adventure in front of me

I am anxiously awaiting instructions knowing that
wherever I go it will eventually lead me home
I am in the unknown inside of me

Knowing the amorphous emptiness
is rich with living not yet lived
and I eagerly await the arrival of the magic spell
which conjures up the form and shape of the new life

It weaves and swirls energy from above and below,
from light and dark, from within and without
creating a magical blend of what has been
destined to be

I am the alchemical vessel, the chalice being stirred
and whipped, folded into myself
again and again until the transformation is complete

What will be the final outcome?
We don't know for sure but it will be good because we
started out with good ingredients.
Perhaps a chocolate mousse!

I Dreamt of the Loss

I dreamt of the loss of my mother.
I felt the sadness and knew her legacy to me
was prayer, the movement forward
and leaving home again
Where was I going?
I don't have a clear picture of where I am going
but felt open and new
and anything felt possible.
A new adventure of possibilities and a sadness at
leaving what I know as home at this time in my life.

"Take your legacy with you and leave so you can
come home again."

Trust in the journey
Trust in your faith
Allow the old to leave
Feel the freshness of the new breeze
as it flows over you, cleanses you,
bringing you to the opening of the newness
coming your way.

Coming into your life

Am I leaving the old critical
and opening to the new loving?
Am I leaving the abandoned for the held?
Am I leaving the fear for the security?
Am I leaving the struggle for the flow?
Am I leaving the adolescence for the adult?
Am I leaving the woundedness for the soul?
Am I leaving the angst and hurt for the love and joy?
Am I leaving youth for maturity, wisdom and peace?
Am I leaving what I can't for what I can?
Am I leaving braced for embraced?

Leaving and beginning
Alpha and Omega
Another journey along the spiral path!

I AM YOUR DARK SISTER

You are a dream, dream sleepily, openly, deeply,
dreaming here in this plane
It is all a dream
You are awakening to a higher deeper source,
listen deeply to this source
Follow it inside
Do what it shows you to do
You are here to make manifest your divine nature
Quiet, listen, slow down your pace, deepen,
hold your place, your inner space.

Deeply ,deeply, deeper
comes the light from the darkness.
Deep abiding black holds the key to life

I am your dark sister
Dark and stoic and grounded
Strong from the centuries of life
I am the life in the rotting decay
I am the soil that germinates new life
I am the darkness that sustains new life
I am the womb that gestates new life

I am the darkness that surrounds and holds until
you're ready to birth anew
I am strong, stoic, strength, solid,
grounded in the earth
Centuries and centuries I have lived
in the darkness in the deepness
I am your Essence, your Soulfulness
Smell my richness, touch my skin,
feel my life, walk in my body
Take communion when you birth my children
I grow them for your life giving, your pleasure,
your sustenance, your survival
All depend on me and I give to you willingly
I share my body with you every day
I remind you of the beauty of God, the cycles of life,
the destruction and rebirth and
the one sustaining presence

Life living in everything
My energy lives in everything
Life force lives in me

Midwife the Spirit

You are here to Midwife beauty from within
Bless It
Coax It
Tug on It
Hold It
Sing to It
Call It out
Cajole It
Smooth It
Soothe It
Craft It
Catch It
Bless It
But Midwife It
You Must!

THE PRACTICE

The practice every day
is to feel, see, hear the goodness
all around me and in me

It is a struggle this day like
every other day here on earth

Feeling the lack
Feeling the joy
Feeling the aloneness
Feeling the connection
Feeling the sadness
Feeling the sweetness
Feeling the disappointment
Feeling the exultation
Feeling the lostness
Feeling the guidance
Feeling the loneliness
Feeling the love

Just feeling and releasing
Just choosing which side to land on

The lack and loss or the abundance and support
waffling, wading, shifting from one to the other
A balancing act of succumbing to neither
Holding the apex in between these states
watching, weighing, knowing I belong to neither

You are being put through an annealing process
Two things melting together
You are being called to know a third aspect
a higher order of being
Burned and transformed into a richer form

You can choose to know
and act from this place of knowing

Struggle
is a part of the
Mystical Initiation

She Is

I once again sit in the quiet
I feel the Mother's presence
moving through me
surrounding me
speaking to me

I am at peace when she is near
I am enveloped
in her mantle
of love and strength
She sparkles
like the night stars guiding me home
guiding me
to her powerful presence
and through her winding path

She is forever
She is eternal
She is reigning
She is love
She is alive
She is blessed
She is abiding
She is comfort
She is power
She is peace
She is gentle
She is grace
She is true
She is light
She is life
She is patience
She is sound
She is sweet
She is body
She is soul
She is spirit
She is divine
She is creation
She is among us
She is between us
She is around us
She is in us
She is
She is
She is

Chapter Six
Resurrection

*We have arrived at the fourth stage in the
Feminine Cycle of Transformation.*

*Here is where we emerge and empower ourselves to
release our truths from the old identity, patterns, and
perspectives that no longer serve us
or our highest good.*

*Resurrection is not for the faint of heart. Here is where
our gifts are freed from their encasement and confines.
Here is where they are allowed to freely come forth.*

*This is where we revel in the release and consciously
begin to feel the beauty of who we are, where we are
tempered by the fires of transformation and solidify
our new form having been made stronger from the
annealing process.*

*Here is where we come alive again,
see and pray for the light to continue to illuminate our
path, blessing us along the way.*

BETWEEN THE HEARTBEAT

Between your heartbeat lies a summons
Do you hear it?

Listen deeply!
Calling me is the summons between my heartbeat
Where are you calling me from?

From the depths of your soul
imploring you to listen
for your next deepest truth

Make room for us to speak to you
Open for what is being summoned

Listen! Listen! Listen!

In the stillness is fear
Soothe it
In the stillness is criticism
Stop it
In the stillness is an opening
Step through it
In the stillness is the Great Mother Universe
Be grace-filled by it

My essence says...it is time for birth
My children say...oh shit!
My sovereignty says...bless us and keep us
My soul says...it is as it is
My prayer is...bless me and keep me!

THE TOMB

Into the tomb
stripped away of all adornments
down to the marrow of my bones
Life's blood revealing the true nature
of my human being
Soul infused, divine inspired, spirit led through the
dark spiral path
Downward inward alone with myself
seeking, finding, curiously looking, admiring,
observing, touching,
seeing the naturalness of who she is
Feeling the nature of her being,
experiencing her in her pure form
Alone unadorned with strategies,
personas, protections

She who lives in the depths surrounded by
the quiet walls of darkness
She who enlightens the quiet,
the darkness with her being
She who knows the truth of her existence is sourced
from the light of the Divine
She who is stripped of all adornments
is purity of love, strength, compassion and wisdom
She who is the midwife of my spirit incarnate

The Journey
It is the purpose
It is the meaning making
It is the process of
Individuation

I really want to listen
to my spirit
my inside life
my pureness of spirit

She who knows how to die
and be reborn

"I know how to die and be reborn"
resurrected from the shame
lifted up from the darkness
holding my wounded selves
tenderly stroking their faces
lovingly whispering to them
that they are divine and
God's creation!

They are welcomed home into the arms of the Mother
forever renewed and returned home as children of God

It is another change in the wheel of life
It is another turn of the wheel
It is another gestation period
It is another owning of who you are
at this stage of life

It is deepening into your Self
It is widening the wisdom of your age
It is creating meaning from a new perspective
It is owning your body, soul and self
as the vehicle to meaningful life

It is embodying your purpose at another level
Bring yourself into the world in another way
Deeper richer refined and relishing who I am

You are a woman transforming, changing,
metamorphosizing into another being
Growing pains, shedding old skin,
experiences, imprints from the past
Born anew!

Sacrifice and Resurrection

Sacrifice
Sacrifice is necessary for new growth
and in order to obtain wisdom
Sacrifice of your innocence your youth
your beauty your physical vitality
is the debt paid for the wholeness
and peace and wisdom
Pruning the unnecessary to shape
and release life's energy anew

Sacrifice your youthful optimism
for gracious joyous truth
Sacrifice your wounds for essence and soulfulness
Sacrifice your striving for accomplishments
for peaceful knowing
Sacrifice your tears of sorrow for inner peace
and tranquility
Sacrifice your childhood yearnings
for intimate woman experiences
Sacrifice your self-doubt and fear
for knowing you can survive
death and destruction and loss
Sacrifice yourself for the God-given that you are

Resurrection
Burning, turning, returning
Flames purifying, burning away,
skin turning to embers, returning to dust, flying
away in the wind
releasing all that does not belong
transforming all that does
into the golden light of the divine child of god
fire transmutes impurities into gold
heat red white yellow flames of fire
surrounding my soul and lifting it out
of its encasement of times past,
of human imperfection
into the pure love of the divine resting
in the soul of your being
a taste of divine knowing,
a drop of divine perfection,
a tinch of divine presence,
married to your soul self, revealed to you
amid the darkness, the emptiness,
the aloneness of resurrection
You are alone in the darkness,
you welcome the taste, the drop, the tinch
of God's presence, for it warms you, envelopes you,
soothes you, reminds you
all is not lost but resurrected

All in good time dear one
All in good time!

Redemption

Angel flying, carrying me home
I have redeemed my Self
I have rescued the innocence from the menacing
Alone, naked, on display for the negative masculine
to exert its power over just by its presence
On display in a glass box, to be seen,
captured and controlled

She is beauty in its raw creative form
Where creation beams out of every pore
She is the divine incarnate in human form
She is the sweet surrender
of the human to its soul senses
She is saved and rescued as she swoops down
to save and rescue me
from my human frailties, defects and devices
We redeem each other!

She is the angel and the innocent
The fragile and the fearless
The frail and vulnerable and the time eternal
She is the small ray of hope and the saving grace
She is the innocence embodied
and the eternal evermore

She is the vulnerable expressed
and the wisdom of the ages
She is the ever-trusting in the ancestors
and the descendant
from the lineage of the loving Sophia
She is the everlasting spark of genius
holding the keys to my divineness
Waiting to be unlocked opened and set free

To be

To make manifest
god's gift
of me

Redemption

The Fallen Warrior

Who is resurrected from the ashes of the dead me?
The Amazon stands over the grave
of the fallen warrior
Grieving the death of the warrior, having no clue
that this warrior is a person
It is only a slave gladiator to the Amazon
to be replaced by another she trains in her ways
The fallen warrior is surrounded in her grave
by her Mother
her lover
her alchemist
her spirit
her soul
They recognize the death as sad but necessary

The Amazon will leave and they will wash
and cleanse the body,
Wrap it in cloth and they will take
the deadened body of the warrioress
and bring her home to be cared for,
nursed, nourished,
not back to, but into her, whole, holy, metanoia self
The sum of her parts

Remembered from the burned ashes
of her former body
Mending, blending, assigning new meaning to the
body and its purpose
Death, destroyed, burned beyond recognition, broken

Broken is
the call to arms
The unconscious motivation to serve the Amazon
at all costs in order to survive like a gladiator slave

"I serve no one"
"I choose who and what I serve"
"I am dead"
To the call to arms
To the serving out of fear
To the negative masculine
To the giving without reason or purpose
To being a slave
To being a warrioress to the Amazon

I am dead
I feel the deadness
I cannot pull up the energy within me
I require nursing of my body
I am in triage

The burned out ashes of my former self
are being gathered and placed in an urn to be kept
safe
as I am tended to and nurtured, nourished, nursed,
into my resurrected self

Shaman Snake Woman

Hiss Hiss
Rattle Rattle
Shake Shake

Hiss Hiss
Rattle Rattle
Shake Shake

I am the bone collector
I am the soul reclaimer
I am the initiated old woman
Who sings over your bones and brings them back to
life
Soul infused
Spirit filled
Divine inspired are thee

Having lost thyself to the tragedies of living and life
I collect your bones
Soul fragments
And truths unspoken
I gather them, tend them,
I sing over them
Calling them to life
After every fall into every resurrection

I am the bone collector
Praying over your bones
That the unique soul imprint comes alive again
After it has died for the hundredth time in
the umpteenth initiations you have endured
My spirit sings you alive again and again and again

Hiss Hiss
Rattle Rattle
Shake Shake

Shake up the old, toss it about and out
of its naiveté and uninitiated self
Slam it up against the wall to be broken open
cracking the old form to reveal the tender DNA,
the marrow, open and vulnerable,
everlasting and evermore,
resurrected from the aging body
that no longer works or fits your knowing being

Hiss Hiss
Rattle Rattle
Shake Shake

Let me sing over your marrow
Let me call the spirits to come for you
Let me send the soul into your bones to gestate,
come alive, pulsate and enliven your skeleton

Let me raise energy to raise you up once again
for this turn of the wheel of initiation
combining the Self, the Feminine and the Soul
emerging anew with new skin
for this new adventure as
this newly birthed initiated female

Hiss Hiss
Rattle Rattle
Shake Shake

Hiss Hiss
Rattle Rattle
Shake Shake

THE WAY OF THE FEMININE

What is your message?
Dear Sophia
Dear Mother

You are a child of mine
You are here to honor the Feminine
To create space for her to flourish
within and in the world
Be who you are meant to be
Listen and see as you always have

The coffin is opening to new life
Returning from the lessons of Hades
"Nothingness" with stronger resolve and learnings

Heed the truth that lives in your cells and your body
That is the way of the Feminine
Practice love every day towards yourself and others
No, you are not perfect
but perfect as you are in your humanness
And because you own that,
you are beautiful in your imperfection
Love is a practice towards yourself and others

You are my Daughter
in the darkness and in the light
Transmutation of both
Integration of all

Beauty is your unwavering commitment to life giving
Beautiful too is you in your process of decaying
disintegrating and releasing
that which you have out lived
An old identity that no longer fits your body

Shedding it like a snake molting its old skin
Emerging with a new identity that is soulful,
old and wiser than ever before
The snake releasing the old covering
and keeping the body
that carries all the wisdom in it.

The darkness is the place of birth
In it we gestate, transform and grow into ourselves
Allowing new life to emerge in our cells

New life, new light, new and old soulful imprinting
that we allow to manifest beyond
in spite of our wounded humanness

Blessed be the darkness as it enfolds
all life and welcomes it home
I am returning my Self to you Mother, to the living
Yet I crave the darkness blessing me with its quiet
wisdom

Hold both within and without as temples of worship
Quiet the self, soothe the self
in the arms of your Mother
in the darkness and light,
hold onto the richness of the darkness
as you step into living the treasures of who you are
into the light of day
Return to it as a place of solitude and renewal and
wisdom giving
As it is so

Return again, return again
Return to the land of your soul
Return to who you are
Return to what you are
Return to where you are
Born and reborn again
Return again

You Are

Good Morning Dear One
I am here with you, above you, below you,
inside you, surrounding you
I am here blessing you and keeping you

You are the keeper of beauty
You are the soundness in the fragile
You are the hallowed in the eve
You are the gentleness in the gesture
You are the welcoming in the presence
You are the compassion in the caress
You are the sympathy in the sigh
You are the love in the expression
You are the truth in the purveyor
You are the warmth in the sharing
You are the electric in the life force
You are the soul in humanity
You are the spirit in the sacred
You are the light in the world
You are the child in the god
You are the son of the father
You are the daughter of the mother

Creation of the universe
Beholder of the beauty
You are bound to be
So live truth and beauty
Forever and always
Amen

Chapter Seven
Rebirth

*This is the fifth and final stage
of the heroine's journey on the
Feminine Cycle of Transformation.*

*Here is where we delight in the newly born being we
are, where we ever so tenderly blow life into the flame
and make it roar with aliveness.*

*Here is where we know our gifts, bring them into the
light of day, live from them, and bless the world with
them by being the man or woman we are here to be.*

*Here is where we love more, honor all, seek
compassion, and bless each, where we learn to live
again from this place of peace and truth and knowing,
where we honor ourselves and others who are
traveling this ancient path.*

*Here is where we love ourselves and each other
from a place of strength and goodness. Here is where
we pray that we can be who we are meant to be.*

TRUTH LIES WITHIN

The truth lives within
Light reveals the dark
Dark illuminates the gifts
Soul is who I am
Love is everlasting
Death is resurrection
Peace is a choice
Compassion is a must
Empathy is love enacted
Wisdom is earned
Living is a journey
I am Blessed

A child will be born to you and it will be holy
Out of the darkness
comes light
Out of illusion
comes truth
Out of sacrifice
comes renewal
Out of resurrection
comes new life
Out of revelation
comes rebirth

Out of creation
comes the newborn unveiled!

Deep within lies the truth
Your truth is your soul speaking
Learn to live from this basic truth
Love serve support know god in you and others
Teach guide counsel create sacred space for others to
know their divinity
This is your purpose your passion
and your soul's truth
You have lived this practice since you were a child
You asked for understanding and god's guidance
You have sought it out and lived the journey
the process and the truth since you were young
What you do is valuable and sacred
How you do it is in the order
of the shamans and mystics
Allow teach guide people to their soul
and the truth of who they are
through love presence and guidance
Bless them and keep them safe and sound until they
can do that for themselves
You are a teacher of the Sophian Order
Sophia's daughter
Mary's sister and
The Divine Mother's devotee

I Am a Note

Listening to my soul
The goal is to live the life of change embrace yourself
at every turn of the wheel of life
Listen for the call of wholeness
and holiness and individuation
At every turn of the decade
there are new lessons to learn
You get to embrace them or
fight them but always integrate them

Who are you at this stage?
An older woman
A woman of wisdom
An unadorned woman of
societal expectations for youth
A woman of forgiveness
A woman of commitment to a higher power
A woman of peace
A woman, more than a girl, yet the fear
and uncertainty of the girl reveals itself at moments

Who Am I?
I am the note on the sheet of music
I am the raindrop on the pane of glass
I am the cloud in the sky
I am the sparkle in the night star
I am the heart in the soul
I am the whisper in the wind
I am the fish in the pond
I am the love in the blessing
I am the leaf in the tree
I am the ripple in the water
I am the light in the window
I am the flame in the candle
I am the beat of the heart
I am the child of the Divine
I am the soul in the body
I am the spirit in the holiness
I am my Mother's Daughter
I am the Divine Feminine,
Advocate,
Embracer,
Beloved
Holder of Beauty!

You Choose

It is not totally dark in here
There is a beam ever so slight of Divine light shining
through the darkest of dark
A thin ray cutting through the darkness
illuminating a tiny spot on the floor
Giving hope that I have not been forsaken and the
divine does and will shine again
With the promise of an illuminated path but alas
not yet
Only the hope is available to me in this moment,
that once again the divine will shed its light
on my path one ray at a time so as to gradually
reveal to me my destiny
and thankfully not burn me to a crisp with
too much light too soon

I am kind
I am compassionate
I am giving
I am loving
I am fun
I am playful
I am smart
I am gorgeous

I am beautiful
I am warm
I am precious
I am lonely
I am hard
I am insensitive
I am too sensitive
I am mean
I am cruel
I am impersonal
I am competitive
I am insecure
I am inadequate
I am angry
I am unsophisticated
I am aggressive
I am judgmental

At times yes you are all of these things!
At times you are all of these things and more!

At times you are divine perfected
At times you are human defective

At times you are whole and holy
At times you are separated and fearful

At times you are none of it
At times you are all of it

At times you embrace the beauty and goodness
At times you let go and succumb to your wounds
At times you dance ever so sophisticatedly
with your soul goodness
At times you break down in frustration
at your novice skill level and learning

At times you are light and dark
beauty and bleakness

At times you are loving and unforgiving

You are!

You choose to live in the energetic play between all
aspects of your being

You choose light over dark
You choose holy over unholy
You choose love over unloved
This is your path!

Dearest Daughter,
May peace be with you and love surround you
always!

Soul Speaks

I listen to the images as they reveal themselves to me
in the aliveness of the moment
Whether they be beauty revealed or the inner turmoil
swirling with change
throwing me about
The images speak to me from my soul

Soul Speaks in me
From me
Flows through me in written form
Flows out of me in words revealed

Expressed from my voice
Soulful imaginal expression
True and honest not sanitized or made pretty
But honest in its form, picture, expression

I am here to do your work
I am here to surrender to my soul's gifts
and express them
I am here to midwife this expression
of my soul's birth

So true soul is extracted from the matter
it was infused into
Bit by bit softening, clearing away,
coaxing out of, emerging delicately
The fragile ancient survivable soul relic
and fragment that has remained
true beautiful and preserved for the millennia

Now to be cleared, polished to a shine
and shared with the world
Where its majestic magic and beauty
will be honored and recognized as a most precious
aspect of the being it belongs to

Honoring the ancestry of ourselves
and the Divine lineage we descend from
Recognizing we are a piece of the Divine spark
of the Divine creator
And from this we can live from, in and
with a sacredness that is befitting our origins
and our true nature in this life on Earth

Know your truth and have the courage to live it!
It will hold you steady in the darkest of times as well
as in the lightest of times

LEGACY

My Legacy
Pure of heart
Challenging this human condition
Walking the path of change
Stripping off old skins
Standing naked in my vulnerability
Seeking anew my rightful place in the world and
in my inner life
Embracing the learning my soul has for me
Luxuriating in the darkest of nights
Reveling in the beauty and richness
of Sophia's wisdom
Radiating from my heart beams of spirit's light
Surrounded by the starlit sky
Reminding me I am as unique as one of the sparkling
stars in the night sky
and I am a wonderful part of this
vast and beautiful universe
Returning to myself with the kiss
of the Great Mother
blessing me in all that I am and do
Amen

THE MIRROR

Beauty is in the world

It is the love exchanged in a knowing glance
between two people
It is a look of sweet admiration when someone sees a
flower bloom into its fullness

It is the wonder and excitement
as we hear the thunderclap
and see the lightning crack down from the heavens
It is the gentle and tender cooing and awes
as we recognize innocence
in the face of the newborn baby

Beauty is all around us
It is within us

It is to be cultivated, tended, and looked upon sweetly,
tenderly and in awe and excitement
For it is the mirror
to us of our own divinity and beauty

Beauty is the sweet remembering of our divine origins
allowing peace, love and tenderness to fill us up with
the truth of who we are

Beauty is all around us.
In us, surrounding us, enveloping us
If only we have the eyes to see, the hearts to know and
the courage to be.

PRESENCE

*The sweetness of being seen and heard is
demonstrated when we take the time to see, know and
hold another in deep abiding presence*

*What beauty we witness when someone recognizes
themselves in the eyes or on the lips of another*

*What vulnerability we witness when someone chooses
to share of themselves in their tenderest of moments*

*What delight we witness when someone allows
themselves to dance their child into being*

*What preciousness we witness when someone
acknowledges their gifts ever so tentatively
and for the first to time*

*What power we witness when someone lands
in the voice of their soul and speaks their truth
ever so soundly*

What beauty we witness when someone comes alive in
their body and honors their god-given gifts

What privilege we witness when we hold each other in
the becoming of our being

Bearing witness to god's gifts
unfolding us as we are meant to be

I Am

All will be well Dear Child of Mine
I am the sweet in the surrender
I am the glimmer in the hope
I am the essence in the fragrance
I am the beauty in the beloved
I am the aliveness in the living
I am the warmth in the embrace
I am the nourishment in the nurturing
I am the twinkle in the eye
I am the crystal clear in the dark night
I am the ringing in the bell tolling
I am the instinct in the intuitive
I am the whisper in the wisdom
I am the creation in the chaos
I am the blooming life in the destruction
I am the Mother in the Universe
I am the beauty in the bestowing
I am the grace in the granted
I am the sanctity in the spirit
I am the answer in the prayer
I am the love in the blessing
I am the form in the formless
I am the spark in the insight
I am the spirit in the everlasting

You are mine to guide, console, champion and bless
You are mine to soothe and whisper words of wisdom
and encouragement
As you walk this spiral path of transformation
As you walk this earth walk
As you die and be reborn,
As you let go, strip off, reclaim and resurrect
Yourself out of the chaos of change

Beloved daughter, I am yours to call on any time
I am always here for you Dear Child of Mine
Sleep well, for I am with you always!
Mother Mary Mater Ma

Chapter Eight
Blessings

*These are the prayers and blessings for someone
who is returning from their dark night travels and
integrating their learnings from the
Feminine Cycle of Transformation.*

*These are meant for someone who is coming home –
home to themselves; home to their loved ones; home to
their truth, beauty, and goodness; home to their inner
truth which is, has been, and will always
be there for them.*

*All any of us have to do is go inward,
listen to the body wisdom that speaks from the still
small voice inside and remember our birthright.*

*It is the home of the Divine Mother
who lives within and in each and all.
All we have to do is come home to her.*

Returning Home

I awaken to the bright Night Star
Shining out of my window
with a tiny star following in its wake
I think of the Divine Mother always and ever present
Guiding us through the darkest of nights,
ever present as the beacon of hope,
the guiding star, the fixed point along the way,
the sparkling presence pointing us toward home

She brings us security, hope and direction
Wherever we may be
we can always go to her and she will be
the light upon our path,
guiding every footstep we take forward,
providing safe passage, secure footing
and guiding light towards our home

Home through the deep dark tangled forest
of cragged thoughts and perceptions.
Home through the vastness
of the caves of our inner terrain
Returning Home
Battered and Battle Weary
Tested and Tempered

Raw and Weathered
Powerful and Humbled
Harried and Hopeful
Hallowed and Relieved
Returning Home to safety and security
with competence and confidence as our guides
Returning home once again
after the age-old journey has been traveled
Returning home for the
Rest
Rejuvenation
Repair
Replenishing
Realigning
Relating
Reconstituting
Rebuilding
Reconnecting
Remembering
Realizing that goodness was recovered and rescued
from the dark and empty places
and carried the Oh! so many miles home
Returned to its rightful place,
sovereignty realized, birthright reclaimed
You are the beautiful gift retrieved
and returned to your Self
Receive the Blessings of your inner King or Queen
for they bless your beauty and your birthright

Returning Home!

Love Talk

Beauty is her presence bringing holiness
in sight, sound and body
Beautiful too is my hearing, feeling and seeing her in
all things as the first light of the morning
breaks the darkness of the passing night
She is the way and the light

Beauty is her flowing nature as it spurns me on to
find holiness within
Beautiful too is this human woundedness as it creates
the sacrifices from which to be resurrected
Beauty is the darkness of the dark night of the soul
as it envelopes and blesses
within the tomb of the eternal return
Beautiful too is the eternal return
bringing loss and release
as it brings me home to all that is soulful in me
Beauty is the peace and wisdom that springs forth
from the depths of my being as it reconnects
with its Godhead, source of all life
Beautiful too is the Gnosis of Sophia as she surrounds
me with her loving presence
filling me in the midst of this dark moon night

Beauty is the awe and calm and majestic reminder
after the storm that
Mother Nature is ultimately our place of worship
Beautiful too is the raw, creative, destruction she
wreaks on us all during the cycles of our life creating
shoots of new life, tender green and strong
Beauty is the blade of grass growing
from a rock hell bent on living life fully
no matter what the circumstances
Beautiful too is my prevailing nature, my unique
soul imprint that has thrived even through these most
challenging of times here on earth

Vulnerability

Beauty is the power of your vulnerability
Tears falling like diamonds from the sky
Joy and sorrow being caught and cherished

Beautiful too is the heart splayed open for others
To see and touch and tend your soul-filled ways

BEAUTY

Beauty is dark and stealthy
Stalking my soul

Beautiful too is the power,
Love and loyalty she empowers in me

Beauty is rich, protective,
Instinctual and raw

Beautiful too is her all seeing eyes,
In the darkness revealing
the feminine rules and ways
Wicked Wicked Wonderful Ways!!!

Soul Song

Beauty is my loving Mother and Father present for
me in the air that I breathe.
Beautiful too is their sacred memory
embedded in my heartbeat

Beauty is the grace, peace and love emanating
from their hearts to mine
Beautiful too is the acts of beauty I see being gifted
to me every day in the blue sky,
the green leaves, singing birds and my husband's
twinkling eyes

Beauty is my gift of acting faithfully
in their presence
Affirming, blessing, loving are all acts of faith
I have been gifted with
Beautiful too are the gifts I receive from the Trinity
Feeling, seeing, knowing and embodying their
presence in and all around me

Beauty is spirit singing my song
in the energy of living
Beautiful too is the living energy creating anew,
always and ever after

Beauty is the chaotic dance of change and growth
Beautiful too is the creative force alive in the chaos,
pushing the dead
out of the branches of the Tree of Life

Beauty is the unfolding of all that has ever been and
the enfolding of all that will never be
Beautiful too is the dark night bringing illumination
to the material stuffed in the cracks, nooks and
crannies of the stoned walled foundation of my soul

Beauty is the cleaning, clearing and polishing of the
old stone walls revealing ancient maps to the terrain
I travel as a soul incarnate
Beautiful too is the deeply rooted presence
of the Divine Mother designing me
in her image and soothing me
with her full, beautiful, beloved nature

PEREGRINE

*Let
The Earth ground you
The sky call you
The sun move you
The moon caress you
as you walk your journey
with spirit!*

HAIKUS

I am a spiral
Woven like a spider's web
Intricate and strong

The great cosmic web
Rewoven as my soul shifts
Creating creation

Underworld unspoken
Middle world alive and present
Upper world calling

Shaman's Path

*

Out of darkness light
Rich black glimmering dark dirt
Gestating new life

The Nigredo

*

Warrior boy lost
Broken rudder drifting, lost
Find your way home please!

Negative Masculine

*

Beloved darkness
Twinkle in the dawn early
Light struggling free

Integration

*

Hold Me Great Mother
Suckle me Create anew
My soul yearns for you

Large nourishing breasts
Giver of light, love and moonbeams
Caressing feminine

Deep embracing light
Enveloping me in your arms
Sing sweet lullabies

May I remember
Your vessel bodily felt
Earth calling "embody"

Your essence of dirt
Smells of creative chaos
Birth your existence

Dear One

*

Blessed be new life
Rising flowering femaleness
Pushing through the dark hard soil

Earth Mother Moon Sister Be
Glowing and flowing embodied
Alive and well in me

Alive and well breathes
New life into your soul song
Sing her serenade

Resurrection

*

Spirit breaks first light
Twilight's breath body stirring
Holy Communion

Communion

*

THE DANCE OF CREATION

Blessed Be
Blessed Be Thee
Blessed Be Me
Blessed Be You
Blessed Be Our World

Blessed be the differences Blessed be the familiar
Blessed be the teaching Blessed be the learning
Blessed be the strife Blessed be the truth
Blessed be the conflict Blessed be the change
Blessed be the contrition Blessed be the forgiveness
Blessed be the separation Blessed be the reconciliation
Blessed be the weariness Blessed be the relief
Blessed be the vulnerability Blessed be the peaceful
Blessed be the chaos Blessed be the creation
Blessed be the dance of the world

Moving from one form into another
until all are felt and the opposite is born anew

The Dance of Creation

SOPHIA'S SANCTUARY

Beauty is your sweet sweet soul
connecting through our breath
Beautiful too is the tender
holdings of your women here on Earth

Beauty is their vibrant light dancing
in the bright of day
Beautiful too are their vulnerable whispers
blessing us with their wisdom

Beauty is the ruby red rising sun
calling us all to awaken!
Beautiful too are the bodacious
bawdy blessed females answering your call

Beauty is our sweet surrender to our original nature
Beautiful too is the deep riches of
Sophia embodied in us

We are so Blessed

I Am the Shamaness

I am the shamaness, witch, healer
I am the warrior, priestess, tracker
I am the nurturer, mother, nourisher
I am the home, hearth and sacred place

I receive the power of love, law, light, life
peace, wisdom, and truth into my soul self
May it guide me always
Amen

DANCE ME INTO LIFE

You are my child, my heart and my soul
My bright and shining star in the midst of the night
darkness
Illuminating the path like a full moon lights up the
night sky
You dear child bring love and peace and guidance
and strength to those who need my presence
Through you light shines again on Earth
Through you love will reign over tyranny
Truth over oppression
Cooperation over power
Through the light that lives in all of you
Love creation beauty
will once again come to fruition in this Earth dance
of polarities
It is as it has always been
A dance over the millennia
There may be death
There may be destruction
There may be tearing away of the old guard of power
over
But within this destruction are the seeds of creation

For out of creation comes
Me
My energy
Love
Cooperation
Mercy
Commitment
Creativity
Aliveness
Joy
Peace
Blessedness
It is the Earth school
To dance Me into life
It is as it is and has ever been for eternity
To dance between the masculine principle gone awry
and the feminine principle into form
The duality of all therefore the dance of forever.

May we heed the call for the Feminine coming.
May we open to her presence
May we call her into form in our being and in the
world
May we act in accordance with her presencing herself
to us and for us
She is the guiding principle being birthed into our
existence again, one more time
May we hold her sweetly, lovingly,
protecting her as we would a vulnerable child alone
here on Earth.

In the hearts of all
In the actions of each
In the beauty of everyone
She is the breath of all life
May we sing her into form
May we pray her into being
May we act in a way that makes her proud
May we welcome her into our home, hearth and soul
May we covet her presence as the coming of love that
she is
Amen

Chapter Nine
An Invitation

*I invite you to create your own connection
to the Divine Feminine
as she lives within each of you.*

*Open to your embodied wisdom
by creating a quiet sacred space from which to allow
the still small voice inside of you a place to speak.*

*For 30 days, write daily what you hear her speaking
to you by answering the following sentence stems, to
cultivate your own special relationship with her.*

*May you embrace the presence of the
Divine Feminine in your being and in your life.*

May you be transformed.

Sophia Speaks

*Take time to quiet yourself and listen to the
Divine Feminine through your body wisdom.
As you inquire and call her into your being,
listen and record her answers to you.*

Sophia Speaks....

I see in you...

I bless in you...

I champion in you...

I love in you...

I pray for you...

Sophia Speaks

Take time to quiet yourself and listen to the Divine Feminine through your body wisdom. As you inquire and call her into your being, listen and record her answers to you.

Sophia Speaks...

What she sounds like in you...

What she sings for you...

What her energy emanates for you...

What she yearns for you...

What she feels passion about for you...

What she prays for you...

What she chants for you in the wee hours of the morning...

What she wears for you...

What she protects in you...

What she loves in you...

What she fights for in you...

What she takes a stand for, for you...

What she soothes in you...

What she blesses in you...

What she reflects to you...

What she dances alive for you...

What she embodies in you...

EPILOGUE
THE NIGHT STAR

I am the bright and shining star
that illuminates the way
for weary travelers on their journey
I am the bright and shining star
that provides guidance and the way
for those lost in stormy seas
I am the bright and shining star
that sparkles with brilliance
in the cold of winter's night
I am the bright and shining star
that hovers over the newly
born babe in times of old
I am the bright and shining star
that directs you home through
the cragged terrain of change
I am the bright and shining star
that showers you with
hope in the middle of the dark night
I am the bright and shining star
that remains forever fixed
in the cosmos as a reminder you are destined to be
I am the bright and shining star
of Divinity blessing you
with God's Light every step along your way

I am the bright and shining star
guiding you home sweet home
to your beauty and your brilliance
I am the bright and shining star
of the Great Mother's
radiance and beauty holding the world
in her loving embrace
forever and always blessing
each and every one of you
along your way
All you have to do is look up into the night sky
and remember
I am always with you...

ACKNOWLEDGMENTS

Beauty is my beloved husband, Craig Tessem, who gently encouraged me to share my writings for the first time with close family and friends. His continued encouragement to reveal my sacred writings has allowed me to share it in the form of my poetry readings and in this book.

Beautiful too is his endless Love, Joy, and Support during the actual living of the journey that this book represents. He blesses me with his presence every day of my life, like the wings of an angel his love lifts up my spirit ever so gently. Thank you, Beloved Husband.

Beauty is my clients who, through the many years, have blessed me with their presence, their faith, their vulnerability, and their beauty.

Beautiful too are their individual essences, blessing the planet with their unique and beautiful soul imprints.

Beauty is my teachers along the way who held so powerfully their student, daughter, sister, devotee with such love and caring.

Beautiful too is the imparting of wisdom and grace where and always when it was most needed. Thank you, especially to Dr. Cara Barker, and also Katherine Fentress and Ron Hering.

Beauty is the many hours of altered states work and Holotropic Breathwork that opened my heart and catapulted my senses into the wisdom of the ages.

Beautiful too is the divine guidance from the Divine Feminine as she lovingly reveals it to me one beautiful drop at a time. Thank you to Jim Frazier for being my spirit compadre.

Beauty is my family, for from these sacred roots come faith in and for the cycles of life and the ethic to work hard and responsibly. This has served me well in life and for that I give thanks to my mom and dad, Jim & Elda Corbit, my brothers and sister-in-laws, Tom & Gayle, Tony & Denise, Tracy & Luz, Rick & Terri, and all my nieces and nephews.

Beautiful too is the black rich soil of the North Dakota farmland I grew up on. I am always and forever anchored to the richness it provides for me, always reminding me of the fertile and regenerative powers of Mother Earth and the Divine Feminine.

Beauty is my extended family, Barbara & Edwin Nielson, Ron & Judy Harlow, and Vanessa & Neil

Hohner, who have loved me from the first time we met and provided connection, love, and laughter aplenty.

Beautiful too is their sweet knowing of me in every stage throughout my life, sometimes knowing better than myself just what I was capable of and mirroring it to me ever so lovingly.

Beauty is my tribe of women who hoot and holler when it is time to champion, who sweetly bless and encourage when it is time to be seen, and who hold and soothe when it is time to be tender.

Beautiful too is their presence, blessing me with their Joy, Laughter, Power, and Love. These women are the best representatives of the Divine Feminine I know of on earth. Thank you, Edy Nathan, Gail Haun, Tinka DiSalvo, Paula Friedland, Francesca Starr, Lynn Parker, and Betty Leuellen.

Beauty is the book crew who guided me, encouraged me, directed me, and showed me the way.

Beautiful too is the ever blessed way they assumed I could do what I did not know how to do. I put myself in their hands and they expertly took me and guided me through to the final destination. I am forever grateful to Andrea Costantine, Nick Zelinger and Donna Mazzitelli for their personal and professional wonderfulness.

About the Author

Lizanne Corbit, M.A. is a licensed professional counselor and a life coach. She has been in private practice as a psychotherapist since 1990. Her passion for spirit, soul and essence has guided her in all avenues of her work. In addition to seeing clients individually, she facilitates women's groups and personal growth workshops and retreats.

Presently, she is facilitating Soul Speaks Groups and Soul Speaks Retreats. She is also sharing the message of the Divine Feminine to audiences and groups through the reading of her sacred writing.

Lizanne lives with her husband Craig Tessem in Denver, Colorado. If you would like more information, you can visit Lizanne's website to see the current listing of retreats, groups and workshops at www.LizanneCorbitCounselingDenver.com.

Lizanne invites you to contact her directly and would love to hear your experiences while reading this book, you may email her at Lizcorbit@yahoo.com.